THE IMPACT OF INFLUENCE

Creating a Meaningful Legacy

L. GLATT

TABLE OF CONTENTS

INTRODUCTION

Our lives span many phases. A large part of our adult life is spent investing in our personal success and securing a stable and secure future for our family and ourselves. We work hard and we start to look forward to the next phase; but what is the next phase? This is the time to reflect on the Legacy you are creating.

Does your Legacy have any influence on others? Having a positive influence on others is personal and powerful. You have the opportunity to make a difference in the lives of others. Not everyone has an interest in leaving a lasting and meaningful Legacy. Those that embrace this opportunity enrich this phase of their lives and bring a sense of goodwill and accomplishment that cannot be measured.

This book lays out basic, practical actions to begin creating your meaningful Legacy. At first glance, you may feel you already have a good handle on some of these ideas; but dig deeper and be honest in your self-reflections on how committed you are to carrying out each action.

Within these pages I have shared some of the opportunities I embraced, the actions to which I committed and messages from those I have influenced. I encourage you to begin your journey into creating your meaningful Legacy.

SECTION ONE – FOUNDATION

> ➢ ACTION ONE – FIND YOUR PASSION

The time has arrived. A new phase in your life is beginning. Anything new and unknown can seem daunting. Where do you begin? My journey began after attending a conference for female executives working in the Criminal Justice Field. The leaders of this conference found a way to unite and inspire us. I returned to my respective organization with a fire to make a difference. My fire focused on building a supportive network for the females within our agency. My passion was to unite all females across the wide expanse of the agency regardless of their position or location. As you can imagine creating something of this magnitude in a male dominated field was certain to face challenges. My commitment and plan to sustain my goal had to be strong.

This is your first step. Find something you have a true passion for that will sustain the ups and downs the commitment will face. Start with a reflective period to consider issues important enough that you would want to guide and inspire others to navigate through them and achieve their best. This first passionate plan of action will be the base of your foundation.

➢ ACTION TWO – BUILD YOUR PILLARS

The pillars that supported and shared my passion were two other women within my organization who had attended the conference with me. We reached out to other key women who we knew would share this passion. Together we created the Women In Partnership Organization (WIP). WIP proved to be a powerful and influential part of our agency. I stayed committed to the success and growth of WIP from its inception until the day I retired from the agency. WIP reached up to 450 female members all within our agency. Keeping the passion and involvement of the many members, took a strong team of women. The need for the main pillars are to give you relief. Sometimes you will find you need a break; that is when one of the other pillars stands a little stronger to carry the load while you recharge.

Creating a network of women across varied positions and work locations proved that we were stronger together and were able to provide each other with much needed support, mentoring and guidance. This is your second step; reach out to others who share your passion who can provide you guidance, support or even join in your plan.

> ACTION THREE – STABLILIZE YOUR BASE

Get the buy in. What is in it for others who can help support your plan? For my plan, I needed the buy in from the highest administration and from the majority of staff who happened to be men. First and foremost is to be professional in your approach. We knew if the staff felt valued and appreciated, the return would be increased morale. Who wouldn't want a better work environment? We were fortunate to receive steadfast support from the top down. When the top leaders make their support and commitment known, it makes a definite statement on the legitimacy and value of your plan. Decide whose support will make your plan more successful. Reach out to those people and take the time to present your plan along with the expected results you hope to achieve.

KEY POINTS

- ❖ Find a passion that is important enough to you that you are willing to sustain the ups and downs required of a commitment.

- ❖ Reach out to others who share in your passion in order to have a strong team and support system.

- ❖ Get buy in from top stakeholders. Their support will help ease over future hurdles.

SECTION TWO – RAISE YOUR INFLUENCE CAPABILITY

➢ ### ACTION FOUR – DEVELOP YOUR ABILITY TO CONNECT

How do you connect? Who you are and how you connect with people will determine the positivity and power of your influence. I developed my ability to influence others over the many years I served in leadership positions.

I remember my turning point; a time that I reached out to someone to help me achieve my goals. The assistance provided to me proved to be invaluable. It was then I realized that I wanted to share all I could with whoever was willing to accept. My definition of success had suddenly changed. It was no longer about my personal success but about reaching out and helping others achieve theirs.

That sounds like a plan, however, there will be no influence if there is no connection. Action Four is about developing who you are and the steps you must take to be on the road to connecting.

ACTION STEPS

BE GENUINE AND HUMBLE

Simply put, this means do not try and be someone you are not. You may think you need to portray a certain image or come across as the most knowledgeable or skilled leader. If you fake it, it will show. If you fake concern, it will have no value. Think about the people you know that try and fake it. They are the last people you would communicate with regarding your true aspirations and concerns. People trust and connect with those with which they can identify. Be you, but be the best you.

DO NOT HOLD GRUDGES

There will be cases where we have crossed paths with someone and the result was not positive. Don't let the past experience stop you from this opportunity to leave a positive influence. Be open and fair to everyone. If you are sincere in your desire to do the right thing, then you must hold yourself above holding grudges.

UNDERSTAND THE VALUE OF EVERYONE

Each person has value both personally and professionally. The majority of people are in support roles. While the tasks they perform may not put them in the spotlight, the project or task would not be successful without their piece of the puzzle being in place. It takes the whole team for the mission to succeed. One person does not do it alone. How you treat others shows your true character.

BE APPROACHABLE

Make eye contact with people. Be the first one to greet people. When meeting someone, set a time you know you will not be distracted. Have interest in what someone is telling you. When you give others your undivided attention, you show you respect them.

APOLOGIZE

Everyone makes mistakes. If you are in a leadership position, your mistakes likely affect a lot more people. If you make a mistake, admit it, own it and apologize. Do not put this off. It must be done immediately. If your apology needs to happen in front of the group, then make it happen. For those affected by your mistake, they know you were wrong. You must be strong enough to admit your mistake and apologize. They will be waiting to hear this from you. If the apology does not come, neither will their respect.

BE WILLING TO GET DIRTY

You've worked your way up. You may be the boss. As the boss, remember that all eyes are on you. Be careful to not let your position go to your head! Remember that no job is beneath you. If you find yourself in a situation where something needs to get done and you are the one who is there and can get it done, then do it. Don't do it so that others see you helping out; you should genuinely want to lend a hand when the need arises. This goes a long way in earning respect.

FOLLOW THROUGH ON YOUR COMMITMENTS

When you build relationships and begin stepping outside your comfort zone you will find yourself with tasks that are on you to complete or follow up on. You must do what you say you are going to do. If you fail to keep your word, you will lose trust.

SHOW APPRECIATION

Be sure when you show your appreciation, you are genuine. Whatever you chose to do, be sure to do it sooner rather than later. It may be an acknowledgement or a gesture, but it needs to have meaning. When you show genuine appreciation, others will feel valued.

BUILD RELATIONSHIPS

Building relationships is vital to your support system. Your relationships should include a variety of individuals. Sometimes there is not an apparent reason for forming a relationship with someone. Don't throw away this opportunity. Once you take the time to nurture the relationship and take the time to learn and share with that person, you will realize how valuable their presence is in your world. Relationships must be given time and attention. You don't wait until you need someone to call them. Take time to break away from the work environment to have quality time with someone. The work is always going to be there. When you break away and spend time with someone in your support system, you will return to work with a renewed energy and positive attitude.

DO THE RIGHT THING FOR THE RIGHT REASONS

You have to ask yourself why you want to influence others. Your reasons should be genuine and sincere. As you build relationships, integrity is key to earning trust and ultimately opening the lines of communication. Always ask if you are doing the right thing for the right reason.

ASK FOR AND ACCEPT HELP

There will be two circumstances where you will ask for help. One will be when you need someone to teach you. You don't know everything but the support you have built around you can help you learn the tasks that you need to be successful. The other circumstance will be when you are trying to accomplish a task or project and need help from others to accomplish all that needs to be done. Be willing to reach out to others but be willing when the coin flips and they in turn ask you for help. When you create a team that works well together and respects each other, it makes for a positive experience that others will start volunteering for in the future. When they volunteer, accept the help!

TRUST THOSE THAT ARE HELPING YOU

Learn to trust others to do what they've said they will do. In the beginning you may have a backup plan, but over time you will learn who you can trust without hesitation and without worry!

PICK YOUR BATTLES

Don't fight every issue. Learn how to pick your battles and learn when to compromise. When you can work with others, they will work with you. When the time comes that you chose to battle, you will be listened to because others will know that you speak up when it is truly important. Your voice and your opinion becomes important and others will now pay attention and seek out your opinion on many matters.

SEEK OPPORTUNITIES THAT FURTHER DEVELOP YOU

Continue to develop yourself and your skills. There are opportunities to turn your knowledge and experience into a seminar. This type of action will enhance your speaking skills, causing you to delve further into your topic of interest and provide you with the opportunity to meet new people who can further enhance your support system. Use the internet as your friend to seek out educational classes, books and publications that will keep you up to date on current trends in your field. The more you know, the more you share and ultimately the more you influence.

SAY YES AND SAY NO WHEN APPROPRIATE

You don't have to say yes to everything and everyone. When you find your passion be sure that the things you say yes to support your goals.

When times arise where you have to say no to someone, be straightforward. Don't keep taking things on for fear of saying no. Others do not know all you are doing. You must communicate.

SHARE YOUR EXPERIENCES – GOOD AND BAD

There are many lessons you have learned as you have journeyed down your path. Those that look to you want to hear about your past experiences, good and bad. Others want to know that the person they see as a Leader may have stumbled or overcome some obstacles along the way. It will help them to know you understand and can guide them as they move along their path to success.

REACH OUT TO THOSE ISOLATED FROM THE MAINSTREEM

Think of those people that are out there holding down the fort and keeping things running. Do you only contact them when you need to speak with them; or do you ever just reach out just to check on them? This is not just about those that work for you. This is about reaching out to those that you know don't have a large support group around them. A simple phone call may be nothing to one person but to these others, it will mean more than you realize.

DON'T LET THE NEGATIVE ATTITUDES HAVE THE STAGE

No matter how hard you try, there will always be negative people and naysayers. They strive for attention and to be center stage; don't put them there. The rewards go to those who chose to move forward in a positive manner. Negative attitudes have no place affecting what is important to you. You can't be a positive influence on those that choose to stay closed off.

LAUGH

Nothing breaks down barriers more than sharing a laugh. This shows you are not a robot but actually a human being! The ability to share a story and laugh about it will create a positive experience with individuals and leave them with upbeat memories of their interactions with you.

SHARE WHAT YOU KNOW

You have experience. Others have helped you achieve success. It's your turn to pay it back. Sharing knowledge and teaching others builds the future of your agency. You won't be there forever but those you have mentored will continue to mentor others.

KEY POINTS

❖ There is no influence without a connection.

❖ To influence others, you may have to take steps outside your comfort zone. Be brave and step out!

❖ Your genuine self will always come through. Be sure you do the right thing for the right reason.

SECTION THREE – EMPOWERING OTHERS

> ### ➤ ACTION FIVE – DEVELOP PATHS TO INFLUENCE OTHERS

You've built strong relationships. You have built trust and opened lines of communication. Your actions are having a positive influence on others. Now you want to do more. You understand the importance of leaving a meaningful Legacy and wonder if there are other paths in which you can make a positive influence on others.

Think back to your initial passion. Whatever mattered most to you must keep your fire burning. Take that passion and find ways to expand it out in new directions.

For me, I continued with the original Women In Partnership Organization but collaborated with others on how we could grow and create new opportunities to reach people. We worked hard and brought in committed supporters to help with each new path. The first path was created from my desire to help others with basic tips for promoting. We rallied all the supervisors that we admired and requested they participate in a project we called Career Builder. After the first year, this project exploded and became a three part seminar spread out over several months.

After several years of assisting over 50 people promote, we turned this project over to younger supervisors to organize and conduct each year. Influence happened and meaningful Legacy was created.

Around this same time, I and the other leaders of our Women In Partnership Organization were introduced to two inspiring and influential women. We were asked to collaborate and put together a statewide seminar for female supervisors working in the Criminal Justice Field. Our planning resulted in the creation of a unique training seminar that allowed participants the opportunity to grow personally and professionally.

We aptly named this seminar STRIVE (Support – Train – Respect – Involve – Validate – Empower). Each female leader attending met peers from across the state and all returned to their respective agencies with renewed energy and a commitment to making their agency better. The success of this seminar resulted in our highest leadership requesting we continue this training as a yearly event.

This new phase of reaching out beyond our agency required the involvement of many of our own female leaders to ensure its success. It was at this time I noticed several female supervisors were working in fields were they had no peers. They had no one to discuss issues with, request guidance, or just give and receive support. I saw the need and created a network in my agency for all female supervisors that chose to partake. Women In Supervisory Encouragement (WISE) was born.

The first thing I discovered when we would get together was that women I thought I knew for many years, I didn't really know. This group allowed us the opportunity to get together and have open dialogue. I was amazed at the strength and commitment of these women. They were inspiring.

The development and on-going commitment to keep the group together and conduct regular meetings was priceless to each of us. We all influenced each other and created our meaningful Legacy.

At the same time, the women who collaborated to create our STRIVE seminar invited me to be a part of an even larger organization in which they encouraged me to become a speaker and to participate in planning future conferences supporting women working in the Criminal Justice Field.

There are many ways to develop paths to influence others. It all goes back to your passion. My passion was to unite all female employees across all departments. I wanted them to understand each other's value, develop professional relationships and support each other through a wide network. I committed to several paths for many years to make this happen.

While this was my passion, I continued with building relationships with everyone that crossed my path, worked with me or reached out for assistance. I knew I was there to support others, regardless of my position.

➤ ACTION SIX – KEEP THE LIFELINE EXTENDED

It doesn't end. When you truly have a positive influence on someone, they want to stay connected. They will seek you out even after you have left the agency. If you did the right thing for the right reasons, then you will keep that lifeline extended. Those you have influenced trust you. They trust you to be honest with them, to give them solid guidance or ask the hard questions, whatever may be needed at the time. Be open to those that reach out. Consider it an honor.

KEY POINTS

❖ Your passion is always the foundation of new paths.

❖ Share your idea with others that can assist you in making the paths a reality.

❖ Keep the lines of communication open, even after you have left.

MY MEANINGFUL LEGACY

I am grateful for the many supportive relationships developed during my career. I was honored to be a positive influence to others. I have included some messages sent to me as I was retiring. I hope you can see some of the actions touched upon in this book within these messages.

∞ There are so many positive things I can say about how she impacted me personally and professionally. We always felt that we were important and that she appreciated the work we did.

∞ She made a point to visit with all of us on a regular basis. She's the type of supervisor who would "roll up her sleeves" and work right beside her staff. She is a great leader, an impression that will stay with me even after she retires.

∞ You left your mark on so many people and I am one of those you made a lasting impact on.

∞ She has been a great mentor to me throughout the years, giving me great advice of what to do, what not to do and mostly encouragement to keep "my person" that I could always count on for honest talk, encouragement and understanding.

∞ You've been there when we needed you.

∞ The respect I have for you can never be duplicated. Your legacy has been embedded into our hearts and minds. You made a DIFFERENCE.

∞ She is a supervisor who will take the time to call you at 0400 in the morning to answer a question and ask how your night is going.

∞ She is open to ideas and understands when you make a mistake and shows you the right way it should be done with sound practical advice. She motivates and challenges you to be better.

∞ A supervisor, a woman of courage to stand up for the right thing, a confident, someone that made me laugh in the hardest of times, a true supporter but most of all a FRIEND.

∞ Know that you left a legacy.

∞ I have been so fortunate to have walked beside you. You taught me something every day. Because of that I believe I have become a better supervisor, confident, supporter and friend.

∞ Unconditional Giving. Strong and Proud.

∞ I never had the pleasure of working directly for her but quickly established a working relationship where I looked up to her and respected her opinion. Even though neither one of us knew at the time what an impact she would have on my life both professionally and personally.

∞ You have been a mentor, supporter and true friend and have had a truly huge impact on my life.

∞ All my respect.

∞ I have always admired how you were a very hard worker, always professional, nose to the grindstone, looking into the future with resolve but balancing it with care and compassion for others.

∞ She is a strong, determined woman who does what she thinks is right despite what others may think. She holds her staff accountable for their choices but does not belittle them for mistakes. She allowed me an opportunity to redeem myself.

∞ Her innovative, inspiring ideas have done great things for the women of this agency. She is a great example of genuine leadership. Her legacy will be felt for many years.

∞ I have obtained a hair sample and will be cloning you for future generations. There will never be another like you. You are smart, FUN, truthful and kind.

∞ I will miss your smile, it is magnetic and contagious. I always felt I could be myself around you. I wish I could have been lucky enough to call you my supervisor. I was still fortunate enough to learn from you.

∞ I will never forget the woman that united us crazy females. What a feat in itself.

∞ She gave me the best advice ever.

∞ I was impressed with her overall knowledge. She was always willing to share that knowledge with anyone that was willing to listen.

∞ She totally cared for her staff and did all she could to make the job enjoyable for them. Every supervisor should model themselves after her.

∞ I had no idea how lucky I would be to have such a wonderful mentor to teach me how to be a good leader. You were there for me.

∞ Because of you, I am who I am today and am eternally grateful for that. Thank you for everything you have done for me. What legacy you have made.

∞ She was the first shining example of leadership I encountered at the agency.

∞ You have been an amazing, knowledgeable role model.

∞ Good mentor and friend.

∞ You have been a true, positive leader.

∞ Thank you for your energy and ever positive attitude. You are a force that will be missed.

∞ Thank you for your leadership and mentorship over the years. We should all strive to be as respected as you are by all around.

∞ Your leadership / mentorship in the WIP and WISE group will be the legacy you leave for countless women who are / and will be working in our environment. This place is a kinder, friendlier, more supportive place for women due to all your hard work.

∞ Your support of me personally has always been seen as a gift and will be a bright spot for me in remembering my career.

∞ Your energy and enthusiasm will long be remembered and your fun-loving spirit and great fun ideas have been a ray of sunshine and a great source of humor.

May this last page

be the first page

in your journey

to an

Meaningful Legacy!